C000064689

The Irish As The Great Temp

Builders Of The Ancient World

Conor MacDari

Kessinger Publishing's Rare Reprints

Thousands of Scarce and Hard-to-Find Books on These and other Subjects!

- Americana
- Ancient Mysteries
- Animals
- Anthropology
- Architecture
- Arts
- Astrology
- Bibliographies
- Biographies & Memoirs
- Body, Mind & Spirit
- Business & Investing
- Children & Young Adult
- Collectibles
- Comparative Religions
- Crafts & Hobbies
- Earth Sciences
- Education
- Ephemera
- Fiction
- Folklore
- Geography
- Health & Diet
- History
- Hobbies & Leisure
- Humor
- Illustrated Books
- Language & Culture
- Law
- Life Sciences

- Literature
- Medicine & Pharmacy
- Metaphysical
- Music
- Mystery & Crime
- Mythology
- Natural History
- Outdoor & Nature
- Philosophy
- Poetry
- Political Science
- Science
- Psychiatry & Psychology
- Reference
- Religion & Spiritualism
- Rhetoric
- Sacred Books
- Science Fiction
- Science & Technology
- Self-Help
- Social Sciences
- Symbolism
- Theatre & Drama
- Theology
- Travel & Explorations
- War & Military
- Women
- Yoga
- *Plus Much More!*

**We kindly invite you to view our catalog list at:
http://www.kessinger.net**

THIS ARTICLE WAS EXTRACTED FROM THE BOOK:

Irish Wisdom Preserved in Bible and Pyramids

BY THIS AUTHOR:

Conor MacDari

ISBN 1564597547

READ MORE ABOUT THE BOOK AT OUR WEB SITE:

http://www.kessinger.net

OR ORDER THE COMPLETE
BOOK FROM YOUR FAVORITE STORE

ISBN 1564597547

Because this article has been extracted from a parent book, it may have non-pertinent text at the beginning or end of it.

Any blank pages following the article are necessary for our book production requirements. The article herein is complete.

CHAPTER XI

The Irish the First Cultural Nation, the Earliest Missionary Teachers, and the Great Temple Builders of the Ancient World

One of the aims of the propaganda for spreading misinformation regarding Ireland was to create an impression, because of a similarity between the customs of the Irish and those of the Hindoos, that the Irish and their customs came originally from the East, or India. Really, on the contrary, this fact only confirms the truth that the Irish gave their customs to the Hindoos during their missionary sojourn in that country. The Hindoos have never been known as a colonizing race, while we have overwhelming evidence to show that Ireland was the greatest colonizing country of the ancient world. They were the real pathfinders of the world. As to the likelihood of a Hindoo migration to Ireland in the past, the author of *Atlantis* says (p. 416): "The Hindoos have never within the knowledge of man sent out colonies or fleets for exploration; but there is abundant evidence, on the other hand, of migrations from Atlantis* eastward." "And how," he asks, "could the Sanskrit writings have preserved maps of Ireland, England, and Spain, giving the shape and outline of their coasts, and

---

* Atlantis is but a fictitious name for Ireland. — C. M. D.

their very names, and yet have preserved no memory
of the expeditions or colonizations by which they acquired
that knowledge?"   Once the plain truth is made known,
the plot of the conspirators becomes evident on all sides,
and the fabricators of spurious history are seen to have
gone to such absurd lengths, among others, as to invent
the fabulous tale of the "lost continent of Atlantis,"
described by "Plato," in order to carry out their purpose
to obscure Ireland's great past.   This great past, if
known, would at once prove to the whole world that
Ireland was the original parent country of learning, the
sciences, and spiritual culture, and the Motherland of
true religion.   This fact is cryptically preserved by
tradition and the myth that schools were established there
by Ollom Ollo, which name means Doctor or Professor
of Science, and indicates the High Hierophant of the
Irish Magian Sun Cult.   It is also alluded to in the story
of "Cadmus" (first one), the first to establish schools.
It is further confirmed by the tradition, veiled in cryptic
form, that long before real or actual schools were established there, a certain Phineas Pharsa (from Phin,
The Sun, and Phar, a man, — a Finician) had established
schools on the plains of "Shinar" (us, we, ourselves).
This fabled place, for the purpose of deception, has been
located in Persia.   This "Phineas Pharsa" and the
"plains of Shinar" is but a secret allusion to the fact
that the Irish Magian Adept Cult of The Sun Worship,
who here on this island were the first men to develop the
latent or potential intellectual and spiritual powers
within themselves, here erected the first schools and laid

the foundation for all the culture, religious and secular, which exists in the world today. This is a fact of fundamental truth, which nothing can shake or destroy. It is attested to on all sides, upon close examination, by the cultural idioms of the Bible and the esoteric truths preserved in the symbolic monuments of The Great Pyramid Group in Egypt and elsewhere in the East. They have left indisputable evidence of this culture in the religious rites and institutions which they introduced here when they brought Sun Worship and civilization to both North and South America. There is the most incontestable proof of this, as will be shown later on.

This purpose to obscure a knowledge of her history and institutions may be further seen in the effort which has been made to create a doubt as to the origin of her round towers and the purpose for which they were erected. There is no doubt whatever, in the writer's mind, but that the Round Tower has always been a *stubborn* fact for them to dispose of, and we are not surprised to find that they have *on hand* records (fabricated since the invasion) which will show that many of those towers were destroyed by an act of nature instead of by the willful acts of ruthless destroyers. One of the methods employed by those fabricators to isolate and minimize Ireland's historical importance is pretty well reflected, as will be noted, in the description given by "Diodorus Siculus," intended for effect on posterity, portraying her as some obscure and little-known island in some remote and unfrequented part of the Atlantic Ocean. Just as if he were introducing a knowledge of her to the world for the first time, or preserving her very name from oblivion. The excerpt which will show this implied mendacity on the part of "Diodorus" will also include as an authority the untruthful Geraldus Cambrinsis. In referring to the latter, Mr. Donnelly is evidently not aware of his untruthful character. So we find him again, among others, in his rôle as an "authority," as was intended. Regarding the Round Towers, those unique and peculiarly original Irish monuments connected with Sun Worship, Mr. Donnelly says: "Attempts have been made to show, by Dr. Petrie and others, that these extraordinary structures are of modern origin, and were built by the Christian priests, in which to keep their church-plate. But it is shown that the 'Annals of Ulster' mention the destruction of fifty-seven of them by an earthquake in A.D. 448; and Geraldus Cambrinsis shows that Lough Neagh was created by an inundation, or sinking of the land, in A.D. 65. . . ." Moreover, we find Diodorus Siculus, in a well-known passage, referring to Ireland, and describing it as "an island in the ocean over against Gaul, to the North, and not inferior in size to Sicily, the soil of which is so fruitful that they mow there twice in the year." Donnelly goes on to say: "He mentions the skill of their harpers, their sacred groves, *and their singular temples of round form*" (*Atlantis*, pp. 416–17).

We here see a conflict of opinion in the statements attributed to "Dr. Petrie and others" and "Diodorus Siculus." We are reminded of a proverb which says: "A lie must have long legs or it will be overtaken." The propagandists have evidently suffered a lapse of memory right here on this point, regarding the antiquity of those towers.

The effect of all this false information has been to set men astray in their quest for a solution as to what country or people we are indebted to for those monuments. Sir John Lubbock (quoted in *Atlantis*, p. 417) says : "They have been supposed by some to be Scandinavian, but no similar buildings exist in Norway, Sweden, or Denmark, so that this style of architecture is no doubt anterior to the arrival of the Northmen." (That is, their arrival in Ireland.)

It seems puerile and absurd that any investigator possessing even the ordinary amount of acumen necessary to deal with the subject of the Round Towers should honestly think, much less circulate the opinion, that the towers were built in Roman Christian times, and give as a reason that it was a place where the priests kept their church-plate. It is, to say the least, disingenuous. The knowledge necessary to the solution of the question of the Round Towers is not obscure or remote from men who, even in a small measure, have given thought to the investigation of things symbolic. The explanation of the Round Tower is simple, and the purpose of its use easy to apprehend. This understanding will at once enable anyone to determine in what country it originated and who the builders were. Those who are responsible for disseminating misinformation know this fact well; the misinformation is but a part of the plan of concealment.

The Round Tower is peculiarly an Irish or Aryan

symbol of the Sun Worship. In their world-wide
migrations to preach the Gospel the Irish erected the
towers in association with their Temples. They are
symbols of the phallus, and represent the creative power
of God, through the Lord Sun Iesa, both in Nature and
in Man. It has a natural, mystical, and spiritual sig-
nificance. The same idea has been borrowed and embodied in the modern church spire. The remains of those
towers are found as far apart from Ireland as India, in the
East, and from Ireland to New Mexico and Colorado, in
the West. The author of *Atlantis* (p. 418) most per-
tinently says : "It will not do to say that the resemblance
between these prehistoric and singular towers, in countries so far apart as Sardinia, Ireland, Colorado, and
India, is due to an accidental coincidence."

It is sometimes necessary in dealing with a shameless
and persistent propaganda of falsehood to speak in a
plain and direct manner, especially against powerful and
subtle agencies which have been able, through means
of the written page as a medium for misrepresentation,
either by alteration or by omission altogether, so suc-
cessfully to obliterate and reduce to an unimportant and
insignificant character the history, or story, of the greatest
nation of ancient times, if not of all time. The commercial greatness of this nation was unrivaled; her
universities and schools of learning, not only in mediæval
times but anciently, made her the "Intellectual Sun of
Europe," as Professor Sigerson of Dublin recently
declared. Without any exaggeration whatever, and
with justice, we may supplement his statement and say

that she was truly the intellectual light of the whole world. Her ethical culture has never been equaled, let alone surpassed, as evidenced by our Bible, which, when rightly understood, with its ideal counterpart in stone — The Great Pyramid Temple Pillar of Iesa — is her crowning glory. So it becomes very apparent why there has been such an amount of feigned ignorance regarding the origin of the Round Towers and the failure of those with knowledge to give out correct information about them. It is absolutely certain and without a shadow of doubt that the Papal Hierarchy at Rome, and its members in Britain and Ireland as well, were in possession of this knowledge, and that they also had a lively knowledge of the long and continuous intercourse between Ireland and the American Continent, or Land of the West. The traditions of this intercourse never died out among the Irish. The old tradition of "St. Brendan" sailing to the "Land of the West" in A.D. 545 * from the foot of the great headland in Kerry which bears his name is but

* Dates are unreliable. "There are eleven Latin MSS. in the Bibliothéque Impériale at Paris of this legend, the dates of which vary from the eleventh to the fourteenth century, but all of them anterior to the time of Columbus" (*Atlantis*, p. 240). These dates are evidently fictitious and spurious, and are, we believe, intended to provide "authentic records" that would show, in case of need, that St. Brendan's voyage was a rare and unusual one and made close to the time of the jurisdiction of the Romish Church rule in Ireland, which, as stated, began in the 12th century. But the alleged date of 545 A.D., which is given as the date of the voyage, even brings it within the time in which the Irish are supposed to have been converted to Christianity by "St. Patrick." These dates are intended as an alibi by which to explain any resemblance which might be discovered later between ancient American religious rites and institutions and those of Roman Christianity.

merely a ray to shed light upon this fact. There is evidence that the fact of this intercourse was a common tradition along the Atlantic Coast of Europe; and it is safe to say that Rome knew of the colonizations made by the Irish on the Western Continent and of the religious establishments which it was their wont to set up wherever they planted a colony. With due caution to the reader to make a proper allowance for the attempt of the Roman Churchman always to connect the Irish with the Roman Church, we will let the Abbé Brasseur de Bourbourg speak on this point. In a note to his translation of the sacred book of the Mayas, the "Popol Vuh" (quoted in *Atlantis*, p. 419), he says: "There is an abundance of legends and traditions concerning the passage of the Irish into America, and their habitual communication with that continent many centuries before the time of Columbus. We should bear in mind that Ireland was colonized by the Phoenicians (or by people of that race). An Irish Saint named Vigile, who lived in the eighth century, was accused to Pope Zachary of having taught heresies on the subject of the Antipodes. At first he wrote to the Pope in reply to the charge, but afterward he went to Rome in person to justify himself, and there he proved to the Pope that the Irish had been accustomed to communicate with a transatlantic world." *

* It may easily be seen from this evidence that, although this Irish Saint is given a Latin name, he was teaching a theory and pursuing a course which was deemed a heresy by the *Roman Church Fathers*, and it is the strongest presumptive evidence that the Irish Church was independent of Rome at that time. If he had been a member of the Roman Church, he would not have dared to preach such open heresy;

In view of the knowledge which we possess today and the belief which is founded upon that knowledge, it is worth while to consider here, if but briefly, some of the circumstances connected with the voyage of Columbus. In the accounts, be it remembered, we have been informed that he sought aid from the Church Fathers. He traveled about from one church establishment to another, and it is said that he went to Rome to seek aid there. However that may be, a junta composed mostly of the Church Fathers in Spain, after hearing his views and beliefs, refused him assistance or approval. This opposition lasted for a number of years, but was later evidently withdrawn, as we find that it was through the influence of a Father Confessor of a Spanish monastery that King Ferdinand and Queen Isabella fitted out the expedition which enabled Columbus to embark upon the voyage westward. Spain at the time, with its King and Queen, was almost completely under the Church influence. We are told that Columbus's reason for embarking on this voyage was an ardent desire to plant the standard of the Cross in the new lands which he might discover and that he believed that by sailing westward he would be able to find a new trade route to the Indies. These reasons which have been given out are specious and may be dismissed as not being the true

and neither would he have had an option as to whether or not he would have gone to Rome. He would have been peremptorily summoned there for his heresy and disciplined. The very fact of his voluntary appearance there proves his independence, regardless of his facts. At the time stated there were yet many Irish monks and scholars belonging to the Irish Church on the European Continent.

motives. As for the desire to set up the Cross, — we
will see that this expedition and subsequent ones, under
the leadership of the priests, destroyed the Cross wherever they found it on this Western Hemisphere. And we
may also set aside as fiction the fitting out of the expedition to discover a new trade route to the East because
the Turks or Moslems dominated the overland trade
route to that part of the world. In the absence of
knowledge, this latter reason has appeared plausible.
In order to sustain this impression as to the object of the
voyage, we are told that the two commercial and trading
republics of Venice and Genoa suffered most by the loss
of the eastern trade route and that they were especially
clamorous for the discovery of a new route to the East.
Now, if this were a fact, why did not these two states,
each comprising a seafaring people equipped with
fleets and eager for commerce and trade, send their
fleets to the West to trade and make discoveries after the
news of Columbus's successful voyage had spread abroad?
They were the two greatest maritime states in the
Mediterranean, if not in Europe, at that time. If they
needed a trade route so badly, would they not have
entered into competition with the other nations for their
share of the trade and spoils? Instead of those two
states, whom we have been told wanted it most, we find
Spain, Portugal, England, France, and Holland monop-
olizing the trade and the spoils of discovery. None of
these nations were better equipped for overseas trade
or voyages than Venice and Genoa, and it is rather surprising that the latter did not engage in the western

trade. If their need were so great, would not the Pope, when he assumed to divide the New World into spheres, allotting one to Spain and another to Portugal, be very likely to assign spheres respectively to those two Italian City States? The whole thing is merely a part of the fabric of lies invented to conceal the real motive for projecting the voyage. Columbus was said to have been a Genoese, but discoveries have been made since which show that he was a Spanish subject, born and bred in Spain. Thus, it is obvious that the alleged reasons for the voyage are false and will not do. They have been accepted heretofore without close examination.

There was another and far more urgent reason for the voyage. But, before proceeding to give the real cause back of it, let us dispose of the excuse of the Turkish or Moslem menace to commerce between Europe and the East, which was but dust for the eyes so that men would not be able to see the real motive. There had been constant commerce carried on between the West and East, not only during the period of time we are dealing with, but long before and since over the land and sea route from the Mediterranean, through Constantinople, and by devious routes eastward. The Moslems have dominated the main eastern overland route for more than seven hundred years. There was a partial interruption to their sway during the Crusades when the Christians held the Kingdom of Jerusalem for a period of eighty-eight years. This kingdom fell in 1187 A.D., and the period of the Crusades came to an end about 1285 A.D. It was not the Turk who stood in the way of commerce

or trade as such. The Crusades were brought on by
Rome, who instigated the Christian nations of Europe
to attack the Moslems in order that she might possess the
so-called Holy Land. The Turks were forced to defend
themselves and the land which had been in their hands
for some centuries. But there was no unsurmountable
barrier to peace if Rome had wished peace, when again
the stream of commerce could have resumed its wonted
flow. The Turks have never abjured trade or commerce.
During the wars of the Crusades, the most frightful
massacres and excesses were committed, due to Christian
fanaticism. Yet, despite all this, the Moslem King
Saladin of Egypt and the Greek Emperor Alexius of
Byzantium had no difficulty in coming to a mutual
understanding and making peace between themselves
and the peoples of their respective countries. But with
the Roman Church it was different. The Fatimite
Caliph of Egypt wanted to make peace with the Roman
Church cohorts, and he "offered to guarantee to all
unarmed pilgrims an unmolested sojourn of one month
in Jerusalem, and to aid the Crusaders on their march to
the Holy City, if they would acknowledge his supremacy
within the bounds of his Syrian Empire" (*Enc. Brit.*,
9th Ed., p. 625). His proposal for peace was rejected.
Rome was out for spoils and possessions to increase her
income and power. The onus belongs to Rome for
whatever of interruption there was to commerce with the
East, and this could have been removed at any time, we
believe, if Rome had earnestly desired it. It can readily
be seen that the demand for a new trade route could not

have been very strong or Rome would have had to yield
to it. So we may dismiss this reason as an invention.
Moreover, if a new trade route was to be found, why look
to the westward for it? We have been taught to believe,
through interested sources, that the western ocean, in the
time of Columbus, was believed to be an unknown and
limitless waste of waters holding the most forbidding and
frightful terrors and peopled by hideous monsters of
gruesome shapes who would destroy anyone venturesome
enough to attempt to go far to the westward. After
the conquest and absorption of the Irish Church, such
fictions may have been spread among the masses by the
Roman Church priests, and in a few generations they
would have found a wide belief. If so, they served a
purpose for Rome for the time being, while she was con-
solidating her conquests in different parts, and strength-
ening her organization for future expansion and growth.
The astute leaders of the church held no such notions
regarding the western ocean.   The mental medicine they
prescribe for the multitude is something apart, and always
has been, from what they themselves partake of.   So, on
that point there is not the least room for doubt; for, if
they believed such silly fiction, it is only reasonable to
suppose that they would not have at any time favored the
project.   That the voyage had another objective than
that given out by the priests, we may well believe.   The
circumstances under which the voyage was promoted and
aided merits a much more extended elucidation than I
am privileged, from the nature of this work, to give here.

Let me briefly call attention to the struggle in which

Ferdinand and Isabella were engaged with the Moors in an endeavor to reclaim the Kingdom of Granada. The completion of this struggle left the King and Queen as exhausted of all means as did the Crusades leave practically all Europe. And more especially did the Fathers of the Church feel the effects due to the Crusades in the loss of revenue from properties and privileges which they had formerly held but which were now taken over by the Kings and nobility to recoup, in a measure, the losses sustained in those wars to advance the interests of the church organization. This state of affairs had a direct bearing on the project of Columbus's voyage and on the final decision to promote it. The resources of Ferdinand and Isabella were so low that she had to pledge her jewels in order to find the means to furnish the necessary vessels and supplies.

The War against the Moors which reduced Spain to such an extremity was waged, in a measure, as much in behalf of the Church — to banish the infidel and reclaim the country for Christendom — as it was to regain the country for the Crown of Spain. The country, as a consequence, was in a terrible state of poverty, and the Church was also financially lean. This state of affairs, coupled with the fear that, owing to the persistence of Columbus in seeking aid which might be granted by some one whom the Church could not control, caused them, after due deliberation, to promote the voyage at that particular time.

That the Papal authorities at Rome had long possessed a pretty good knowledge of the Irish intercourse with the

Western Continent we may well believe; this knowledge they obtained from the Irish priests as stated by the Abbé Brasseur de Bourbourg. In fact, it would have been next to impossible to have kept this knowledge from them, as Ireland was the greatest maritime nation in the world and *the one* with which Rome had the longest struggle we have any record or tradition of. So it goes without saying that the hierarchy at Rome knew that the Irish Church of Iesa Chriost had established Christianity, or Sun Worship, on the Western Continent. This knowledge must have been confirmed by the Irish priests who were brought into the Roman Church organization at the time of the suppression of the Irish Church.

So, when the project of the western voyage was first proposed, it was looked upon with ill favor by the Church Fathers, because they considered it inopportune and the time inauspicious. They feared that the voyage would lead to the discovery and revelation of facts before the whole world which would be damaging to the Church. Therefore, they tried to dissuade Columbus, under various pretexts and discouragements, to give up the idea, and in every manner possible, by argument, ridicule, and false logic, to convince him that he held erroneous ideas concerning the shape of the earth. By a display of "superior learning" they sought to convince him that his theory and beliefs were alike fallacious. In the light of what transpired, it seems that those men, when they found that they could not dissuade Columbus from his purpose, parried for delay, and, in the meantime, they formulated a plan of policy by which they could prevent intelligence of any damaging facts, which might be discovered, from spreading abroad. It was only after this decision was made, we believe, that enough information about the Western Continent and the great wealth which existed there was made known privily to Ferdinand and Isabella. And it was this information which decided her to sell her jewels, her very last available assets, to finance the expedition. Considering the war in which the royal pair were then engaged and the sacrifices which they had already made to advance the interests of the Church, it is not reasonable to suppose that the priests would have encouraged or advised her to part with her jewels, her last penny, to back a wild and foolish proposition, as they had hitherto held it to be. But they now gave both her and the King assurances that the outcome of the voyage was a certainty beyond merely the ordinary hazards of the sea.

In view of the knowledge in our possession, a fact may be stated here, and one of no little importance in this connection; and that is that a companion of Columbus on this voyage is listed on the rolls as "William, the Irishman, from Dublin." In view of the importance which attached to this enterprise, and what was openly staked upon it by his royal patron and secretly expected of it by the Church Fathers, it is but natural to suppose that men of the best nautical skill and knowledge were secured to assist Columbus. So it is only fair to assume that this person was sea-wise in the knowledge of the Irish mariners, who were formerly the unrivaled sea voyagers of the world, from time out of mind, their nearest competitors, but far inferior in range, being the Norse of a later day.   This Irishman William may have previously made such a voyage himself, which might account for his being with Columbus on this voyage.   If such was the case, no record of it would have been allowed to exist.   The systematic suppression of facts, which is almost beyond belief, of the history of Irish achievements, is most shameless and barefaced, carried on by agencies already mentioned.   It is the plainest fact that Ireland's history has been written by her enemies.   However, it is important to note that an Irishman was one of the personnel of that voyage.   He was of the race of seamen who made voyages across the western ocean and had a constant intercourse with the people of this American Continent from the time of the Bronze Age (See *Atlantis*, Art. "Bronze Age in Europe," pp. 237, 238, 246, 249, 259, 260, 266, 267).   It is a fair conjecture, to say the least, that he brought some particular and special knowledge to Columbus and was familiar with the seafaring traditions of his race.

The Church Fathers, in all essentials, practically ruled the Spanish Kingdom and were the closest advisers of the King and Queen.   Those shrewd men, crafty strategists, with a world perspective for their organization, knew of the Irish Church colonization on the opposite side of the Atlantic; and that it was from there that the priests of the Irish Church obtained the gold and silver for their church service and for the ornaments of their symbolic monuments, Pyramids, Temples, Towers, Obelisks, and Dallans.   Ireland itself, so far as known, never yielded more than a small amount of those metals, and they were dedicated to the use of the Sun Worship. The policy decided upon, judging by what actually occurred, was to place a close censorship upon the voyage. The same policy was applied to subsequent voyages, and all along we find the priest accompanying every voyage and in the van of every expedition.

He was there to observe everything discovered and to bring back a report to his superiors, and, more especially, to take note of the religious state and conditions which were found existing in the Western Land. He was there also for the purpose of mutilating and destroying whatever evidence might be found that would be injurious or damaging to the claims of the Roman Church. This evidence was found in abundance everywhere, as will be shown.

All things considered, there is no other hypothesis but this outstanding fact upon which to account for the sack and ruin of temples and altars, monuments and symbols, as well as the destruction of cities, coupled with the awful killings and massacres committed by the Spaniards, dominated by the priests, upon a highly civilized, peaceable, and practically unarmed people. They received the Spaniards as friends, even as the traditional "fair Gods" (bearded white men), the Irish Magi, returning to them again, as was expected and promised, — they received them with open hospitality and welcome. The recompense they received in turn was frightful and savage. They were slaughtered, with the result that in a few short years the population was reduced in numbers, their leaders killed off, their civilization destroyed, and their temples and religious institutions ruined. This happened not only in Mexico, but also in Yucatan and Peru. It is not my purpose to go into this phase of Spanish policy extensively here, much less to treat of the enslavement of the natives; but only to show the underlying motive that was back of such action on the part of the Spaniards. This will be seen by what the priests discovered.

They found here, as was expected, an abundance of proof of the Irish or Aryan connection with the religious institutions in Mexico, Peru, and elsewhere on this American Continent. They were practically the same in both North and South America. It was the Irish Sun Worship or Christianity which prevailed among the civilized inhabitants of both continents. The name Cuzco, the Capital of Peru, the Seat of the Sun Worship in South America, testifies to their establishing a colony there. For Cuzco is an Irish Name of the Sun God (from Cais, meaning an eye, haste, a twist or turn — whirling — a stream, love, virility, — of the Sun in Spring). The Sun God Casga is still worshiped to this day, not only in Ireland, but throughout the entire Christian world, on "Domhnaig Casga" (Easter Sunday), the day of the Risen Sun in Springtime. The City of Cuzco was the Seat of the Ainca (Inca) or head of the Sun Worship in the Southern Continent. These facts alone, even in the absence of other direct, positive, and indisputable proof, should leave no doubt whatever as to who discovered and civilized ancient America.

I will briefly mention some only of the rites and customs which the Spanish priests found here in the religious worship of the people. They found, among other things, the worship of The Holy Virgin Mother and Child. She was worshiped as the Mother of God. The annunciation that she was to be the Mother of the Savior was made to her by an angel, and the Child became the Crucified Savior who died on the Cross. This savior fasted for forty days on a mountain and was tempted by Satan, the same as Iesa (Jesus). They found here the Sacrament of the Eucharist and Communion. They also found the institution of prayer, confession, belief in the forgiveness of sin, fasting, and the doing of penance. They found the practice of Baptism, where the infant was baptized with water and the Sign of the Cross. This water washed away sin and the child was born anew. They found the Irish institution of religious houses both for virgin women who dedicated their lives to the service of God, and for men who led a chaste and pure life. They found the Cross and Crucifix held in great veneration everywhere in Mexico, Yucatan, and in Peru. In brief, I may say that they found in practice here in America about all of the religious rites which were brought here by the ancient priests of the Irish Church of Iesa, and which were identical with what is now called Roman Catholic Christianity. They formulated this religion originally and spread it around the world to all peoples who were capable of receiving it. It is not surprising at all if, during a period of thousands of years, it became affected with some slight changes. It would be strange if it did not.   Time has effected change in all religions.

Here is what the Rev. J. P. Lundy says of the rite of baptism and the manner in which it was given: "American priests were found in Mexico, beyond Darien, baptizing boys and girls a year old in the Temples at the Cross, pouring the water upon them from a small pitcher." In South America the natives took baths as a religious rite to cleanse away sin, and a very natural, but for all a remarkable, thing about it is, that the Irish name of those baths have survived for those thousands of years and have come down to us to confront and refute those despicable frauds who have stolen the fruits of the Great Irish Apostles, who were the first to preach the Gospel of "The Word" to the whole world.   Those baths were called "Opacuna," or the "bath of sins," that is, the bath for the cleansing of sin.   The Irish word for sin is "paca," and "pacuna" means "the sins."   These facts leave no room for doubt as to whom we owe the civilization of Mexico, Yucatan, and Peru, and elsewhere on this American Continent.

A Spanish priest, the Rev. Father Acosta, in speaking of the religious rites and customs of the natives, says: "The Indians had an infinite number of other ceremonies and customs which resembled the law of Moses, and some of these which the Moors use, and some approaching near to the Law of the Gospel, as the baths of *Opacuna*, as they call them; *they did wash themselves in water to cleanse themselves from sin*" (*Bible Myths*, p. 323).

The Rev. Acosta seemed to marvel at these things, and, as if to account for their presence among the Indians, as he calls them, gives it as his opinion that Satan usurped these things and gave them to the natives for his service, as he wished to be worshiped with the things which were used in the worship of God (*Bible Myths*, p. 404). His opinion is just so much nonsense and was intended for his ignorant and superstitious followers of that age. They also found that the natives had the doctrine of the Trinity from the Irish Sun Worship. One of the Mexican Divinities was Tlaloc (Talac — the Irish Sun God). The names of the persons of the Trinity are easily recognized even in this our day, as Irish names of The Sun God, namely, Yzona, — Iesona; Bacob, the genitive of Baal; and Echia, which is but a variant of Eac, The Sun God, with an ending added to it to formulate a name. And with all this we find that the Mayas of Central America worshiped the Irish Sun God Kukulcan (Cuculan). Can all this be attributed to mere "accidental coincidence," or can any of these be called an "isolated fact"? No, they belong to a series of facts constituting a mass of evidence which establishes beyond all doubt the racial identity of the authors of our ancient American civilization. It has just been announced (April 19th, 1923) that in the ruins of the City of Chichen-Itza there has been discovered the statue of Chac Mool, the famous Tiger King of the ancient Mayas. This is none other than a statue of the personified Sun God, still bearing his ideal mythic title Chac Miol (from the Irish Cac, each, every, all, the whole, universal). As Iesa is the personal

Savior of each and every man, He is also the Universal Savior of all. And Miol, an animal — any animal — is an ideal term which the ancient Irish priests applied to the Sun. Chac Mool is called the Tiger King because of the fact that the tiger (jaguar), a fierce native animal, is King of the jungle of Yucatan. This is after the Irish ideal in our Bible, that the Sun is the Heavenly Lion, and the earthly lion is the King of the animal world. It is from this ideal that we get the term "Lion of the Fold of Judah." What stronger proof could be adduced or wished for with which to confound the falsifiers of history, Roman or British, and those who follow their lead? In the press news of the day is published the opinion of an archaeologist that the date of the structure of the vast architectural remains of Chichen-Itza goes back to the 7th century A.D. Such an opinion will bear revision in view of the convincing evidence of a vastly greater antiquity. Where, we may ask, can it be shown that any other such like structures have been built in any part of the world since the seventh century, or within even the period, so-called, of the Christian era? No, those buildings are many thousands of years older than some would have us believe.

The Cross and the Crucifix are specially and peculiarly identified with the ancient Aryan Sun Worship and Christian Church of Iesa Chriost. They are symbolic of the crucified Sun in the heavens and of His Human counterpart, His Spirit in Man, in the flesh. This identification of those symbols with the ancient Irish, who were the original missionary race of the world, makes it easy to understand why there is such a similarity in the names of the Hindoo Savior Christna and the Christian Savior Christ. They are one and the same and came from the same source. And this explains also why Brahminism, Buddhism, and Christianity so nearly resemble each other — they are all due to those missionaries of the Irish first Church of Christ. It has always been a puzzle to honest investigators to account for this striking resemblance. If the exploits or past history of the ancient Irish people were chronicled in our histories, there would have been no difficulty whatever in accounting for those facts. The same policy of destruction, suppression, and alteration which was pursued in Ireland by Rome she also put into execution on this Western Continent. In Mexico, as elsewhere, anything that was found resembling Christianity was destroyed, if it was possible to do so. The Roman priests destroyed all the books they could find, and those they preserved they altered. "They deleted whole chapters from the writings of the native historians who wrote the history of Mexico" (*Bible Myths*, p. 199). Everything written by the natives was subject to an inquisition of the Spanish priests.

But, despite all the destruction of literature and monuments by the Spaniards and others, there is enough left to fully prove the connection between the Irish or Aryans and the discovery and settlement of this Western Continent. There is a tradition among the natives of Central America that the first of their people came from over the sea to the eastward, and were white men and bearded; and the beard has been proverbially worn by the ancient Irish, — they are so portrayed to us. And what is more, it has been found that one of the oldest of the Maya races, the Chiapenec, after the lapse of many thousands of years, has in its language many words of the same meaning and almost identical with "Hebrew." This is according to a Mexican scholar, Sr. Melgar, in "North Americans of Antiquity," p. 475 (quoted in Donnelly's *Atlantis*, p. 234). He has compiled a list of words of both languages which bears out his contention. And it has been shown, according to Donnelly, that there is a similarity between the Maya and the Phoenician alphabets, which is not surprising, in view of all the facts. When we consider that the Irish were the "Phoenicians" and also, as we have shown, that the "Hebrews" were the priestly cult among the Irish race, it makes very plain the identity of those "three peoples" as being *one and the same*. Investigators have noted the relationship between the "Hebrews" and the "Phoenicians," attributing it to the spread of Hebrew culture and influence among the latter. This seems to be as far as they have been able to go toward enlightening us. They have left us to infer that this connection was due to the two peoples occupying two adjoining sections of country, the Hebrews occupying the interior pastoral country and the Phoenicians the seacoast. Those investigators seem to have accepted the false story of history at its face value and to have drawn their inferences accordingly. The "Phoenicians" and the "Hebrews" were one and the same race, as much so as two brothers living in the same household or father and son in the same family.' These are but "trick" names for the Irish race; Ireland was their seat, capital, and home country, not the eastern coast of the Mediterranean or Syria. This exposes a major deception of history and surely will help to give a clearer perspective of the past and a quickened realization of the fraud which has been imposed upon us. This deception has caused no end of confusion among scholars and investigators. But the announcement of the identity of those "three races" as being *one* is a fact, given out in these pages for the first time, with a positive assurance of truth. The disclosures made here will be of aid to future investigators and philologists in tracing and accounting for the changes which have been made in the three alphabets, said to have belonged respectively to the Irish, Hebrews, and Phoenicians. They are but variations of the one. We have good reason to believe, and it has been so stated, that there have been changes made in the Irish alphabet since the advent of the Latin influence of Rome into Ireland. The research work and explorations which have been made, with the excavations now going on, at the immense ruins in Mexico and Central America, if properly appraised by unbiased and capable investigators, will without a doubt correspond with the facts set forth in these pages. The very character and nature of these ruins, — Pyramids, Sphinx, and temples at Palenque near the City of Mexico and at Uxmul and Chichen-Itza in Yucatan, and others elsewhere in America — are sufficient evidence to establish the authorship of those vast, impressive, and inspiringly instructive remains. Those first religious rites and ceremonies which were found here by the Spaniards are peculiarly of Irish origin, and have been identified with their early Christian Sun Worship from the most ancient times.

The Irish were the inspired authors of Christianity, which is plainly evident from what has been unfolded herein, and their rites are still observed in the disguised Christian Sun Worship of the present day.* It all goes to show that there has been a deception practiced on the Christian people of the world, a terrible and a cruel deception. The reason for it is no longer a secret. And while those early Masters, who formulated those rites and, as well, the ethical and spiritual principles which we find embodied in the myths and allegories of our Bible, were born as Irishmen, of the Irish race, they were really for the world at large. They labored for all humanity. They carried the Divine Message of God's Truth and the Brotherhood of Man around the world, East and West, North and South, and gave freely to such as were able to receive. To those great teachers we are indebted for our culture; we owe more to them than to any other. They cannot, and they must not, be denied this acknowledgment. Their works are spread through-

* A few days ago (March 18, 1923) an Episcopal clergyman gave in his church in New York City a service and chant after the manner of the Egyptian Sun Worship, and, as reported in the press of the day, he called the attention of the congregation to the purpose which he had in giving such a service. He said it was to show "the unity of all religion." I admired his candor. If he explained anything further to his congregation, he was not so reported in the article referred to.

out the world and bear a correspondence that is unmis-takable.   They built on so grand and imposing a scale as to proclaim to us of today their fidelity and loyalty to their Exemplar and Ideal Savior, The Sun God, whom they conceived as the Logos and Creator of all.   And in honor of Him, for His glorification and worship, they built those great and magnificent Pyramids, towers, obelisks, Sphinx, and temples.   In brief, their works and ideals can be recognized everywhere, from the rock-walled temple ruins of the Angkor Wat in distant Cambodia to Siam, from Ellora and the Cave Temple of Elephanta in India to the islands of the Pacific, from Ireland to Egypt, from Syria to Peru, Yucatan, and Mexico.   The character of their works cannot be mistaken.

These facts are so clear that they cannot be mistaken or set aside; they are convincing and positive proofs; they proclaim to the world that both the religious insti-tutions and the civilization which existed on this Western Continent for thousands of years were brought here by the priests of the ancient Irish Sun Worship and religion of Iesa Chriost, The Sun God.

This is the end of this publication.

Any remaining blank pages are for our book binding
requirements and are blank on purpose.

To search thousands of interesting publications like this one,
please remember to visit our website at:

http://www.kessinger.net

CPSIA information can be obtained
at www.ICGtesting.com
Printed in the USA
BVHW050751040122
625371BV00008BB/910